What We Eat

Sara Lynn & Diane James
Illustrated by Joe Wright

A **TWO-CAN** BOOK
published by
THOMSON LEARNING
New York

Our bodies need food to make them work. Food gives us energy and helps us to grow. All living things need food. Some animals, such as cows, eat only plants. Other animals, including people, also eat meat.

Plants are living things and need food too. Unlike animals, plants make their own food, using sunlight, water, and air.

Keeping the Balance

There are many foods to choose from. To keep our bodies fit and healthy, we need to eat different kinds of food. Eating too much of one kind of food and not enough of another is not good for us.

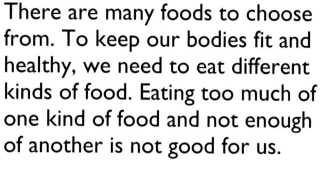

fat and oil

sugar and sweets

cheese, milk, and yogurt

eggs, meat, fish, beans, poultry, and nuts

fruit

vegetables

bread, cereal, rice, and pasta

Look at this food pyramid. The foods at the top of the pyramid should be eaten in small quantities and not very often. But the foods at the bottom should be eaten daily. Eating a balanced diet helps keep your body healthy.

4

In some countries lots of people grow their own food. They raise their own animals too. Have you ever grown anything to eat?

If you could travel around the world you would find that people in different countries have different ways of cooking and eating food. In some countries, the people eat mainly grains and vegetables. In places near the ocean people may eat more fish than meat. And some peoples eat snakes and beetles.

Food & Animals

Animals provide us with many types of food. Not only do we eat meat and fish, but we drink milk from cows, goats, and sheep and eat eggs laid by hens.

Milk can be turned into many other foods. Butter, yogurt, and cheese are all made from milk. Can you think of something very, very cold that is made from milk?

Eggs are a very versatile food because they can be cooked in so many different ways. You can use them to make omelets, scrambled eggs, and poached eggs. They are also used for making cakes and cookies.

Breakfast

If you start the day with a healthy breakfast you will have plenty of energy. Try making some delicious muesli. You can make it the day before you need it and leave it in the refrigerator overnight.

Get ready...
1 1/2 cups oatmeal
3/4 cup plain yogurt
3/4 cup milk
Fruit, nuts, and raisins

Get set, go!
1 Mix together the uncooked oatmeal, yogurt, and milk. Leave the mixture in the refrigerator overnight.
2 The next morning, add some fruit, nuts, and raisins.

Grains

Farmers grow grain crops in huge fields. Wheat is a very important grain. It gives us the flour we need to make bread. It is also used to make cakes, pasta, and different types of breakfast cereals. Whole grains make food crunchy.

Farmers cut their grain crops every year using combine harvesters.

flour

bread and cookies

rice

oats

barley

Rice is another important grain crop. In some countries, people eat it at every meal. Rice grows in warm places and needs lots of water. It can be steamed, fried, or baked.

pasta

Animals eat grains too! Farmers often feed corn to their cows, sheep, pigs, and chickens.

No-Cook Pizza

You have probably tasted a hot pizza covered with melted cheese. But did you know you can make a pizza that does not need to be cooked? You can use many different types of cold food to make this pizza.

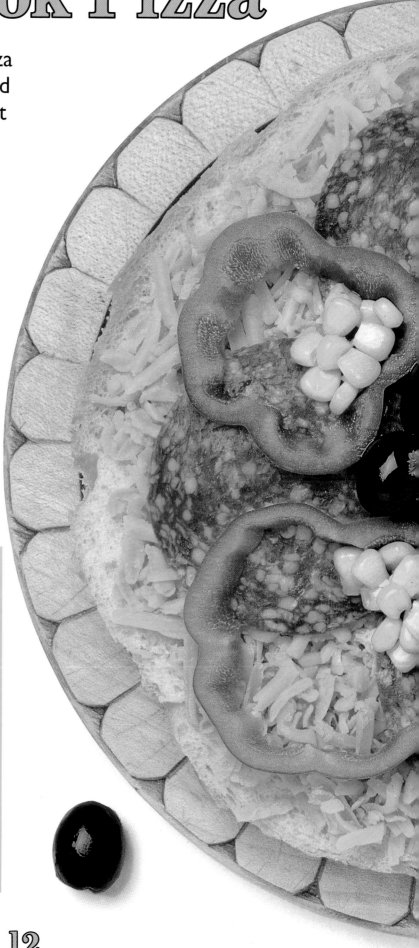

Get ready...
Large, round loaf of bread
Salami, ham, or fish
Tomatoes and peppers
Sliced or grated cheese
Canned corn and olives
Lettuce and parsley
Butter or cream cheese
Chopping board, knife, and grater

Always ask an adult to help when you are using a knife.

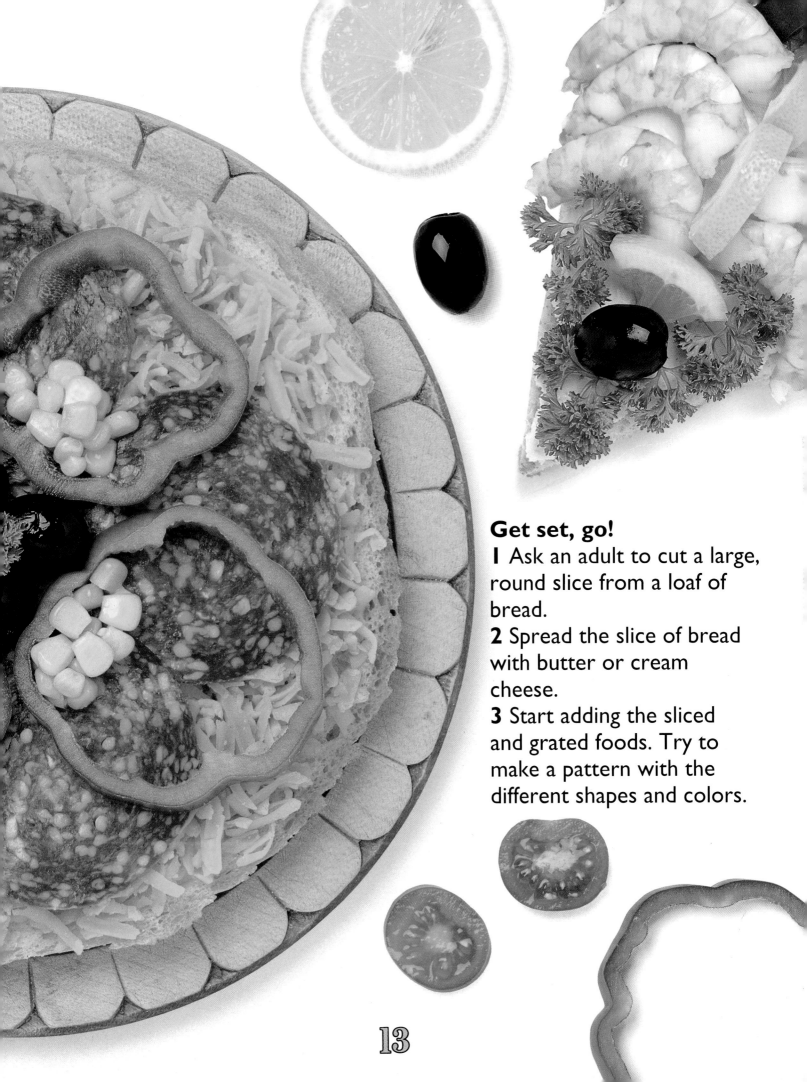

Get set, go!
1 Ask an adult to cut a large, round slice from a loaf of bread.
2 Spread the slice of bread with butter or cream cheese.
3 Start adding the sliced and grated foods. Try to make a pattern with the different shapes and colors.

Fruit & Vegetables

A fruit is the part of a plant that contains its seeds. Seeds grow into new plants. Some fruits grow on tall trees and some on low bushes.

Some fruits, such as bananas and coconuts, grow best in hot countries. They are sent by planes and boats to other countries. Which fruit do you like best?

apple

fig

dried fruit

tangerine

strawberry

banana

green beans

peppers

broccoli

Strawberries grow above the ground. Potatoes and onions grow below it. Sometimes we eat the leaves of vegetables, such as lettuce, and sometimes we eat the roots, such as carrots.

potato

onion

eggplant

zucchini

Salad vegetables, such as lettuce and scallions, can be eaten raw. Other vegetables, including potatoes, taste better when they are cooked first.

Print It!

Get ready...
Fruit and vegetables
Paint
Colored construction paper

Get set, go!
1 Ask an adult to cut a section from a piece of fruit or a vegetable. Look at any seeds you see inside. We used potatoes, cauliflower, apples, and carrots. Try to find vegetables that have an interesting shape.

2 Use a thick brush or sponge to cover the cut surface of the vegetable or fruit with fairly thick water-soluble paint.
3 Press the fruit or vegetable, paint-side down, onto a sheet of colored construction paper to make a print. Try making a pattern using different shapes.

Make a Salad

Some people think that salad is boring. But you can add all kinds of things to salads to make them colorful and healthy to eat. Think about the food pyramid when you are choosing your ingredients. Remember, it is important to keep the balance right. Don't be tempted to drown your healthy salads with dressings, which contain a lot of oil.

Get ready...
Salad Kebabs
Kebab sticks
Small tomatoes
Grapes
Cubes of cheese

Get ready...
Fruit Salad
Cooked rice or pasta
Orange segments
Walnuts
Cress
Raisins

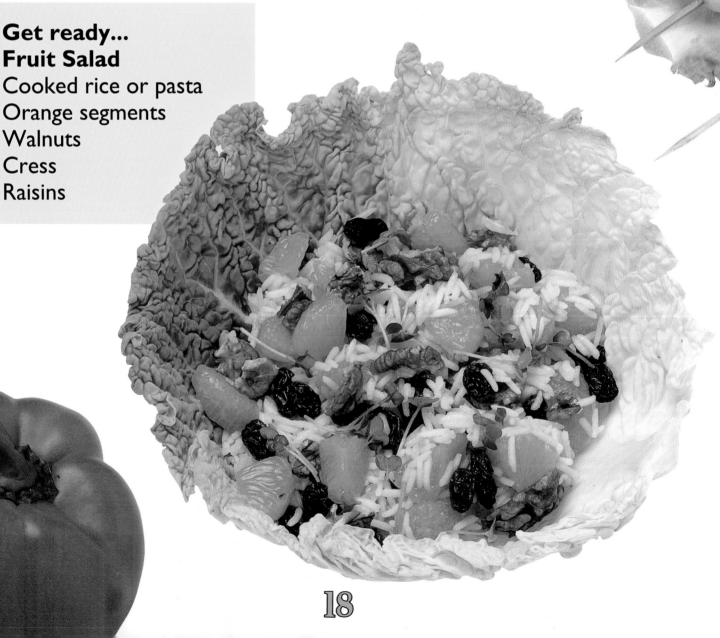

Get set, go!

1 Gather all your ingredients. Wash and dry the vegetables and fruit.

2 Ask an adult to cook pasta or rice for you. Make sure it is cold before you use it in your salad.

3 Chop all the large ingredients into bite-size pieces. Things like raisins, nuts, and olives can be left whole. If you are making kebabs, choose food that will not crumble easily.

4 Arrange the ingredients in a bowl or in large cabbage leaves like the ones we used. Look at the pictures here to get some ideas.

Get ready...
Carrot and Bean Salad
Grated carrot
Cottage cheese
Red lettuce
Kidney beans
Croutons

Far Away

A lot of the food we eat is grown in countries a long way away and transported here. The big picture on this page shows a food market in India. Perhaps you have seen some of these vegetables in your local grocery store?

These women are planting rice seedlings in a flooded field in Japan. Their big hats protect them from the sun.

Bananas grow in hot countries. Sometimes the enormous leaves are used to build roofs for houses and to make bags and mats.

This girl is picking tea leaves. The fresh green shoots are left to dry in the sun. Tea is made by pouring boiling water over the dry leaves.

Chocolate

It's hard to believe, but a chocolate candy bar was once part of a tree!

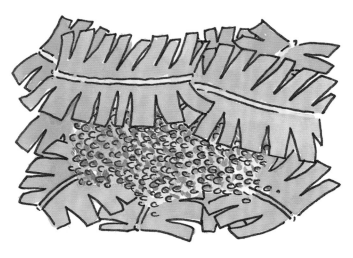

2 The pods are cut from the tree and split open. The beans inside the pods are piled up under banana leaves for a few days. Then they are left to dry in the sun.

I Chocolate comes from the pods of cocoa trees. These trees grow in places where it is very hot and wet.

3 The dried beans are put in sacks. They are taken by trucks and ships to factories all over the world where chocolate is made.

4 When the cocoa beans arrive they are cleaned and roasted. Now they smell like chocolate! The beans go through a grinding machine, which turns them into liquid. Sugar and fresh milk are added.

5 The liquid chocolate is poured into bar-shaped molds and left to cool. Sometimes other things like fruits and nuts are added. When the bars are cool another machine wraps foil and paper around them.

6 The wrapped bars are put in boxes and delivered to the stores where you buy them.

Cookies

When some foods are cooked, they look completely different than they did when they went into the oven. Sometimes they change in size, sometimes in color, and often both ways! Try making some delicious cookies so you can see the changes for yourself.

Do the cookies feel different?
Do they smell different?
Are they the same size and shape?

Get ready...
1/4 cup crunchy peanut butter
1/4 cup margarine
1/8 cup plus 1 tspn brown sugar
1/4 cup granulated sugar
1 egg
1/2 cup self-rising flour

Get set, go!
1 Use a wooden spoon to mix together the peanut butter, margarine, and the brown and white sugar.
2 Sift the flour. Beat the flour and the egg into the peanut butter mixture.

3 Roll the mixture into small balls – about the same size as walnuts. Place them apart on an ungreased baking sheet.

4 Ask an adult to bake the cookies in an oven at 350°F for about 10 minutes. Put the cookies on a rack to cool.

Shopping

The next time you go shopping, look at all the different ways that food is sold. Some food comes straight from farms or gardens and is sold fresh. Some food is frozen and stored in large refrigerators at the grocery store. Frozen food lasts longer than fresh food. You can also buy food in cans. Some canned food can be kept for a long time.

Can you find...

How many different kinds of fruit can you find in the big picture? And how many different vegetables can you spot?

Find the man selling fish. Where do you think the fish have come from?

Look for things that you would need to make a delicious pizza.

Picture It!

Look in magazines and newspapers for pictures of food. You will also find pictures on can labels and other packaging. Pick a theme, such as fruit, and make a collage.

Get ready...
Magazines and
    newspapers
Labels from cans
Empty food packaging
Cardboard
Scissors and glue

**pictures cut
from magazines**

Get set, go!

1 Ask an adult to help cut out your food pictures.

2 Lay your pictures on a piece of sturdy paper or cardboard. Move them around until you are happy with the way the picture looks.

3 Glue the pictures onto the piece of paper or cardboard. We drew a plate on the cardboard first and then stuck the fruit on top.

Quiz

1 What different types of food do we get from animals?

2 How many things can you think of that are made from wheat?

3 Can you think of three different ways of cooking eggs? What is this chef making?

4 What are these children eating?

6 Can you name these plants? Which parts of the plants can you eat?

5 How many of these different fruits can you name?

31

Index

Photo credits: p. 2-3, 8-9 © Fiona Pragoff; p. 7 Bruce Coleman, p. 20 Pictures Colour Library, p. 21 (top) ZEFA, (bottom left) ZEFA, (bottom right) Pictures Colour Library p. 10-11,12-13, 14-15, 16-17, 18-19, 22-23, 24-25 Toby.

Design p. 16-17, 28-29 Hannah Tofts

First published in the United States in 1994 by
Thomson Learning
115 Fifth Avenue
New York, NY 10003

First published in 1992 by Two-Can Publishing Ltd.
Copyright © 1992 Two-Can Publishing Ltd.

Printed and bound in Hong Kong

Library of Congress Cataloging-in-Publication Data
Lynn, Sara.
What we eat / Sara Lynn & Diane James: illustrated by Joe Wright.
    p. cm. – (Play and discover series)
    "A Two-Can book."
    Includes index.
    ISBN 1-56847-141-6
    1. Food – Juvenile literature. 2. Cookery – Juvenile literature. [1. Food.
2. Cookery.] I. James, Diane. II. Wright, Joe, ill. III. Title. IV. Series.
TX355.L96 1994
641.3 – dc20   93 – 35627

Answers

p. 6
Q. Can you think of something very, very cold that is made from milk?
A. Ice cream.

p. 26-27
Q. How many different kinds of fruit can you find in the big picture?
A. There are 9: bananas, tomatoes, grapes, oranges, lemons, pears, strawberries, melons, and apples.
Q. How many different vegetables can you spot?
A. There are 5: cauliflowers, carrots, cucumbers, potatoes, and garlic.
Q. Where have the fish come from?
A. The sea

p. 30-31
1 Meat, milk, eggs, butter, yogurt, and cheese.
2 Flour comes from wheat. It is used to make cakes, pasta, bread, and breakfast cereal.
3 You can make omelets, scrambled eggs, and poached eggs.
The chef is tossing a pancake.
4 They are eating rice.
5 There are 8: apple, blueberries, tangerine, grapes, strawberry, banana, raspberries, and kiwi.
6 Beetroot, strawberries, carrot, and lettuce. You can eat the leaves of the lettuce, the roots of the beetroot and carrot, and the fruit of the strawberry.